# Benjamin Franklin

## Inventor and Patriot

## Carin T. Ford

**Enslow Publishers, Inc.**

40 Industrial Road           PO Box 38
Box 398                          Aldershot
Berkeley Heights, NJ 07922   Hants GU12 6BP
USA                                UK

http://www.enslow.com

**Library of Congress Cataloging-in-Publication Data**

Ford, Carin T.
   Benjamin Franklin—inventor and patriot / Carin T. Ford.
     p. cm. — (Famous inventors)
   Summary: Profiles a man whose childhood love of reading and desire to know about everything led to a multifaceted career as an inventor, scientist, printer, and statesman.
   Includes index.
   ISBN 0-7660-1859-8
   1. Franklin, Benjamin, 1706–1790—Juvenile literature. 2. Statesmen—United States—Biography—Juvenile literature. 3. Inventors—United States—Biography—Juvenile literature. 4. Scientists—United States—Biography—Juvenile literature. 5. Printers—United States—Biography—Juvenile literature. [1. Franklin, Benjamin, 1706–1790. 2. Statesmen. 3. Scientists. 4. Inventors. 5. Printers.] I. Title. II. Series.
   E302.6.F8 F596   2003
   973.3'092—dc21

          2002000487

**Illustration Credits:** Enslow Publishers, Inc., pp. 1, 21; Independence National Historical Park, p. 24; Library of Congress, pp. 3, 4, 6, 7, 8, 9, 11(T), 11(B), 12, 13, 14(T), 14(B), 16, 17, 18, 21, 22, 23, 26, 27, 28; © Theodore Presser Company, Used by Permission of the Publisher, p. 19.

**Cover Illustration:** Library of Congress; Liberty Bell courtesy of Independence National Historical Park.

# Table of Contents

Benjamin Franklin

# Chapter 1

# Boyhood in Boston

**B**enjamin Franklin went to school for only two years. But he had a love of reading that began when he was a very young boy.

Ben read whatever he could put his hands on. He started at one end of his father's bookshelf and went through every book. Ben wanted to learn about everything.

One day, Ben Franklin would be known

throughout the world as a scientist, an inventor, a printer, and a statesman. He would become one of the most important men in United States history.

Ben was born in Boston, Massachusetts, on January 17, 1706. At that time, Massachusetts was one of thirteen American colonies ruled by England.

Ben was the fifteenth of seventeen children. His parents were Josiah and Abiah Franklin. Josiah Franklin ran a shop where he made candles and soap. In the early 1700s, before electric lights, everyone needed candles for light.

From an early age, Ben loved books and reading.

Boston was a busy town full of tradesmen. There were cobblers, bricklayers, carpenters, leather workers, and more. But for young Ben, the most exciting place to visit was Boston's harbor. At that time, it was the busiest port in North America. Ben liked talking to the shipbuilders as well as the sailors.

He also enjoyed swimming. To swim faster, he made paddle-like flippers out of wood to use on his hands and feet.

When Ben was eight, he was sent to school. He was a very good student, and his father hoped that one day, Ben would be a minister in a church. Instead, by age ten, Ben had to start working in his father's shop. He cut wicks for candles and poured hot melted fat into molds for soap.

Ben hated making candles and soap. Josiah Franklin

Ben was born in this house in Boston.

**As a boy, Ben loved to visit the Boston Harbor.**

began to worry that Ben might run away and become a sailor. So, when Ben was twelve, his father sent him to work with his older brother James, who was a printer.

Ben often stayed up most of the night reading. He loved to write, too, especially poems and stories. When James started publishing a newspaper, Ben secretly wrote some articles. He signed them

"Mrs. Silence Dogood" and slipped them under the door of the print shop at night.

Still, Ben wanted to do more with his life. When he was seventeen, he decided to strike out on his own. There was only one way to do this, Ben thought.

He ran away.

Young Ben sold copies of his poems in the city streets.

# Chapter 2

# Printer for the Colonies

Leaving Boston, Ben traveled south by boat and on foot. Tired, dirty, and hungry, he finally arrived in Philadelphia, Pennsylvania.

Ben quickly found work as a printer. After a few years, he was running a print shop of his own.

Ben knew that if he wanted to be a success in his business, he must show that he was a good, honest man. So he dressed in plain clothes. Often he pushed a wheelbarrow loaded with papers through the streets. People could see that he worked very hard.

Ben decided to start a newspaper. It soon became the best paper in the colonies. He wrote stories about fires, murders, and accidents. There were also jokes and poems.

Ben became the official printer for Pennsylvania, Delaware, and New Jersey. It was his job to tell people about new laws and to print paper money.

On September 1, 1730, Ben Franklin took Deborah Read as his wife. They had three children: William, Francis, and Sarah. Deborah helped run the print shop and took care of the children. Sadly, Francis died of smallpox when he was just four years old.

Ben and his wife, Deborah.

In Philadelphia, Ben opened a print and book shop.

Ben began publishing a yearly almanac starting with 1733. This was an important book in colonial times. It was filled with useful information, such as weather forecasts and calendars. Ben called it *Poor Richard's Almanack*. He included many wise sayings, which are still famous today:

A PENNY SAVED IS A PENNY EARNED.

EARLY TO BED AND EARLY TO RISE,
MAKES A MAN HEALTHY, WEALTHY, AND WISE.

**Ben built his own printing press.**

Ben worked hard in his shop. He also cared about improving his mind and body. He drank water instead of tea. He believed in fresh air and lots of exercise. In the 1700s, these habits were very unusual.

In 1736, Ben was elected to the Pennsylvania government. Soon he also became the local postmaster. He was so good at this that he became postmaster for all the colonies.

**Poor Richard, 1733.**

AN

# Almanack

For the Year of Chrift

## 1 7 3 3,

Being the Firft after LEAP YEAR:

And makes fince the Creation    **Years**
By the Account of the Eastern *Greeks*  7241
By the Latin Church, when ☉ ent. ♈  6932
By the Computation of *W. W.*  5742
By the *Roman* Chronology  5682
By the *Jewish* Rabbies  5494

*Wherein is contained*

The Lunations, Eclipfes, Judgment of the Weather, Spring Tides, Planets Motions & mutual Afpects, Sun and Moon's Rifing and Setting, Length of Days, Time of High Water, Fairs, Courts, and obfervable Days.

Fitted to the Latitude of Forty Degrees, and a Meridian of Five Hours Weft from *London*, but may without fenfible Error, ferve all the adjacent Places, even from *Newfoundland* to *South-Carolina.*

By *RICHARD SAUNDERS*, Philom.

PHILADELPHIA:
Printed and fold by *B. FRANKLIN*, at the New Printing-Office near the Market.

To improve his mind, Ben formed a club called the Junto. The members talked about politics, science, religion, and poetry.

With the club's help, Ben started America's first public library. He also began Philadelphia's first fire department, and he set up a school that later became the University of Pennsylvania.

Ben helped start the first public library in the American colonies.

## Chapter 3

# Experiments with Electricity

**B**en's print shop was very successful. By the time he was forty-two, he had earned enough money to stop working. He could spend all his time reading, studying, and exploring the world of science.

Ben had always been interested in observing the world around him. Now he turned his attention to electricity. In colonial times, electricity was a mystery.

People did not understand what it was or how it could be used.

Ben wondered about lightning. Was it nature's form of electricity? In 1752, he and his son William set up an experiment to find out. During a thunderstorm, Ben flew a kite with a metal wire on top. He tied a metal key to the end of the kite string, and he held the key in his hand. When lightning struck the kite, the electricity traveled down the string to the key. Ben felt a shock. Luckily, the electrical charge was not too strong—or he might have been killed.

**Ben was always reading and learning.**

**Experimenting with a kite helped Ben learn about lightning and electricity.**

Ben became famous for his experiments with electricity. To talk about what he learned, he came up with new words—such as *battery*, *charge*, and *electric shock*. He also created a lightning rod to protect buildings from lightning. The rod directs electrical charges safely into the ground.

Ben did other experiments, too. In one simple experiment, he discovered that dark colors absorb heat, while light colors reflect it. This is why we wear light colors to keep cool on a hot, sunny day.

He studied earthquakes, ocean currents, fossils, math, and medicine. In honor of all his work, Ben received special degrees from Harvard and Yale universities. The Royal Society of Medicine in London awarded him a gold medal.

Ben also created the Franklin stove. It gave more heat than fireplaces and used less fuel. His other inventions include bifocal eyeglasses, a machine that pressed clothes, laboratory equipment, and the odometer—which could measure the distance a wagon traveled.

Ben was a musician, too. He played the violin and the harp.

**Ben was interested in fossils likes these bones from long ago.**

He invented an instrument called the glass armonica. It was made of spinning glasses. When he rubbed his fingers on the glasses, the armonica made music.

Ben did not want to earn any money from his inventions. He said that ideas should be shared freely for the good of all the people.

Of all his inventions, the glass armonica made Ben the happiest. He loved the music it made. The famous composer Wolfgang Amadeus Mozart wrote music for this instrument.

# Chapter 4

# Preparing for Revolution

**B**en was smart and hardworking, plus he had a sense of humor. He was one of the most respected men in Philadelphia. When a meeting was called to help settle troubles with the American Indians, Ben was asked to attend.

England ruled all the American colonies. Yet each colony was separate and made some of its own decisions. Ben said that the colonies should join together. Then they would be a stronger force against the Indians.

The idea of uniting the American colonies was new. The colonists did not like it. Ben's plan was turned down.

In 1757, Ben traveled across the ocean to London, England, to meet with the English lawmakers. He asked for help with some of the colonies' problems.

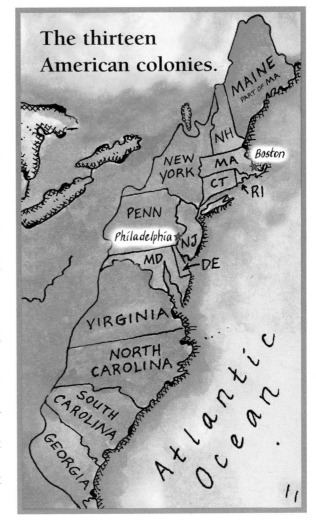

The thirteen American colonies.

For most of the next eighteen years, Ben lived in England, speaking up for the colonies.

As time passed, the American colonists decided they were not happy about having a country so far

away telling them what to do. They no longer wanted their colonies to be run by England.

Ben sailed home in 1775. Although he was seventy years old, Ben was still working hard to help solve the problems of the colonies. He had hoped they could break away from England without fighting. But above all, he wanted the colonies to be a free country.

**Ben used this picture to show why the colonies needed to work together. Each part of the snake is named for a colony. For example, V is Virginia. The parts must join, or the snake will die.**

Leaders from all thirteen American colonies decided to hold a meeting. They wanted to talk about how to win their freedom from England. Ben was a member of this group, called the Second

Continental Congress. The men said that the colonists must form an army. They chose George Washington to lead the soldiers.

The next year, 1776, Thomas Jefferson wrote the Declaration of Independence. This important paper stated that the American colonies should be free and independent. Ben Franklin made small changes where he thought Jefferson's words needed to be clearer or stronger. Thomas Jefferson said that Ben might have been allowed to write the whole

**Ben, standing at left, helped work on the Declaration of Independence.**

paper himself, but everyone was worried he would put in too many jokes!

In 1776, the Liberty Bell rang in honor of freedom. Today, the bell is on display in Philadelphia.

Ben liked to joke, but his skill as a statesman was taken seriously. In 1776, he was asked to go to France. The colonists knew they would need help to win the Revolutionary War against England. They wanted Ben to speak to the French leaders.

Ben did not want to travel to France. But he knew that the colonial army badly needed guns, food, and clothing. So he sailed to France. "I hope our people will keep up their courage," he said as he left his home once again.

# Chapter 5

# Diplomat for America

The trip to France was dangerous. The Atlantic Ocean was filled with English warships. Ben sailed on the *Reprisal*, which captured two English ships during the journey.

When Ben got to France, he felt tired and ill. But he was famous, and the French people gave him a big welcome. They admired him as a scientist and an author. They liked his plain clothes and said that the fur hat he wore was very "American."

Pictures and statues of Ben were everywhere. His face was painted on clocks, vases, and pocketknives.

Ben talked to the French leaders about supplying ships, guns, and ammunition. Finally, in 1778, they agreed to help the Americans. Spain and Holland soon offered aid as well.

Ben enjoyed a big welcome in France. He asked the French to help the American colonies fight against England.

With the help of the French, the Americans defeated England three years later. They had won their freedom in the Revolutionary War. Ben Franklin played a major role.

Ben returned to Philadelphia at the

26

age of seventy-nine. He was given a grand welcome, with church bells chiming, a gun salute, and a huge crowd to greet him.

Ben was pleased that the colonies were now united— as he had suggested many years before.

The colonists cheered when Ben returned home to Philadelphia.

Soon Ben was elected president of Pennsylvania. (Today, that job is called governor.) He also went to a meeting to write the new nation's laws—the U.S. Constitution. He was the oldest member there. Because of his poor health, Ben had to be carried about in a chair.

Ben made one last effort to improve the country. He wanted to end slavery, but he did not succeed.

Ben had owned and sold slaves, but he knew it was wrong. One person should not own another person.

Ben still enjoyed inventing things. He created a rocking chair with a fan attached for hot days, and a long pole that could pull books from high shelves.

But he was old and tired.

Benjamin Franklin died at the age of eighty-four on April 17, 1790. More than twenty thousand people attended his funeral.

**Ben Franklin became world-famous as an inventor, a scientist, a printer, and a statesman.**

Ben had grown up in a poor Boston family. Through hard work and a lifetime full of learning, he became one of the most famous men in the world.

1706~Born in Boston, Massachusetts, on January 17.

1718~Works for his brother, a printer.

1723~Goes to Philadelphia, works as a printer.

1730~Deborah Read becomes his wife.

1733~First edition of *Poor Richard's Almanack*.

1736~Is elected to the Pennsylvania government.

1752~Flies a kite in a storm to prove that lightning is a form of electricity.

1757~Travels to London, works there for many years.

1776~Back in America, helps write the Declaration of Independence.

1787~Helps write the U.S. Constitution.

1790~Dies in Philadelphia on April 17.

**bifocals**—Eyeglasses with one part for reading and another for seeing far away.

**cobbler**—A person who makes or fixes shoes.

**colony**—An area ruled by a far-away country.

**Declaration of Independence**—The historic paper in which the American colonies state their freedom from England.

**electrical charge**—An amount of electricity.

**electricity**—A kind of energy. It is used to power lights and machines.

**politics**—The workings of government.

**postmaster**—The person in charge of mail service.

**Revolutionary War**—A war from 1775 to 1783 in which the American colonies fought for freedom from England.

**statesman**—a leader in the government.

# Learn More

**Books**

Adler, David. *A Picture Book of Benjamin Franklin.*
New York: Holiday House, 1990.

Fritz, Jean. *What's the Big Idea, Ben Franklin?*
New York: Paper Star, 1996.

Krensky, Stephen. *Ben Franklin and His First Kite.*
New York: Aladdin, 2002.

**Internet Addresses**

Benjamin Franklin
<http://sln.fi.edu/franklin/>

Ben's Guide to U.S. Government for Kids
<http://bensguide.gpo.gov/benfranklin/index.html>

The Electric Ben Franklin
<http://www.ushistory.org/franklin/index.htm>

# Index

## A
American colonies, 6, 20–24, 27
American Indians, 20, 21

## B
bifocal eyeglasses, 18
Boston, Massachusetts, 6, 7, 8, 10

## D
Declaration of Independence, 23

## E
electricity, 15–16
England, 6, 20, 21, 22, 24

## F
first public library, 14
France, 24, 25, 26
Franklin, Abiah (mother), 6
Franklin, Ben
   birth, 6
   childhood, 5–9
   death, 28
   diplomat, 24, 26–27
   education, 5, 7
   experiments, 16–18
   inventions, 17, 18, 19, 28
   marriage, 11
   musician, 18–19
   postmaster, 13
   president of Pennsylvania, 27
   printer, 10, 11, 12, 15
   scientist, 16–18
   statesman, 20–24
   writing, 8–9, 11, 13
Franklin, Francis (son), 11
Franklin, James (brother), 8
Franklin, Josiah (father), 6, 7–8
Franklin, Sarah (daughter), 11
Franklin, William (son), 11, 18
Franklin stove, 18

## G
glass armonica, 19

## J
Jefferson, Thomas, 23
Junto, 14

## L
Liberty Bell, 24
lightning, 16
London, England, 18, 21

## M
Mozart, Wolfgang Amadeus, 19

## O
odometer, 18

## P
Philadelphia, Pennsylvania, 10, 12, 14, 20, 26, 27
*Poor Richard's Almanack*, 13, 14
printing press, 13

## R
Read, Deborah (wife), 11
*Reprisal*, 25
Revolutionary War, 24, 26

## S
Second Continental Congress, 22–23
slavery, 27–28

## U
University of Pennsylvania, 14
U.S. Constitution, 27

## W
Washington, George, 23